The knights have died

at the hands of feminism

Phillip A. Johansen

Editorial Anuket

Contents

Introduction

Chapter 1. The Birth of Chivalry: Origins and Tradition

Chapter 2. Evolution of Chivalry Through the Centuries

Chapter 3. Chivalry in Modern Society: A Declining Vestige

Chapter 4. Feminism and the Redefinition of the Modern Man

Chapter 5. The Woke Movement: Dismantling Traditional Codes

Chapter 6. Is This the End of Chivalry or a Rebirth? Final Thoughts

Introduction

"A true knight is one who, being one, does not care whether he is one or not."
The Tango of the Old Guard, Arturo Pérez-Reverte

History of the so-called knights is a complex narrative that traces the evolution of a moral and social code governing the conduct of men in medieval Europe, spanning roughly from the 5th century to the late 15th century.

Initially rooted in the martial traditions of the early medieval period and the sociopolitical landscape of feudalism, chivalry grew to embody ideals of loyalty, courage, and honor, influencing not only military conduct but also cultural and literary productions of the period, such as the romanticized tales of King Arthur and the intricate code of courtly love.

As the concept matured, it developed into a formal Code of Chivalry that outlined expectations of knightly behavior, emphasizing virtues such as courtesy, bravery, and generosity.

This code was not a set of formal laws, but rather an informal set of norms shaped by the cultural values of the time. The rise of chivalric orders, such as the Order of the Garter and the Order of the Golden Fleece, further institutionalized these ideals. However, they too faced scrutiny as military realities evolved and the nature of warfare changed.

Controversially, ideals of chivalry began to wane in the late medieval period, affected by changes in warfare, the rise of a mercantile middle class, and growing disillusionment with romantic visions of chivalry depicted in literature. Critics such as William Worcester lamented the decline of genuine chivalric values, suggesting they no longer reflect contemporary social realities.

Despite this decline, the legacy of chivalry continues to resonate in modern ethics and cultural narratives, fostering ongoing debates about its relevance and interpretation in contemporary society.

The notion of chivalry, rooted in Western history and culture, has for centuries been an ideal that defined relationships between men and women. This code of conduct, which exalted courtesy, respect, and protection towards women, has undergone profound transformations over time. In recent decades, the emergence of feminism and the rise of social movements such as the woke have called this traditional concept into question, generating an intense debate about its validity and relevance in contemporary society.

In this book, we will explore the historical evolution of chivalry, from its origins in the Middle Ages to its adaptation to new social realities. We will analyze how this ideal has been influenced by cultural, political, and economic changes, and how it has been reinterpreted over the centuries. We will also examine the criticisms that feminism and other social movements have leveled against chivalry, arguing that it represents a form of paternalism and oppression towards women.

A central aspect of our analysis will be the tension between traditional chivalry and the ideals of equality and autonomy defended by feminism. Is it possible to reconcile these two contradictory approaches? What implications does the disappearance of chivalry as a social norm have for gender relations?

Finally, we will explore the impact of the woke movement on the conception of masculinity and femininity. How has this movement influenced the way men and women relate to each other? Has it contributed to greater equality or generated new forms of polarization?

Through critical and rigorous analysis, this book seeks to offer a panoramic view of chivalry and its place today. Our goal is to foster an informed and constructive debate on gender relations and to explore the possibilities of building a more just and equitable future for all.

Chapter 1
The Birth of Chivalry:
Origins and Tradition

Chivalry, as a concept, has deep roots in medieval history, although its vestiges have endured throughout the centuries. Emerging in Europe in the High Middle Ages, chivalry was not merely a set of courteous and ceremonial gestures; it was a code of conduct that structured the lives of knights, those warriors of the nobility destined to protect their land, their king, and their religion. However, chivalry transcended the military to become a social norm that influenced the way men should behave with their peers and with women.

Origin and historical context

The origins of chivalry date back to the sociopolitical landscape of the medieval period, which spans approximately from the 5th century to the end of the 15th century. Initially, the concept of chivalry developed from the medieval epic tradition, particularly in the context of the "French Question," which focused on tales such as the Chanson de Geste, which celebrated the exploits of Charlemagne and his knights.

The Rise of Chivalric Culture

Knights, characterized as mounted, armored soldiers, began to appear in the 8th and 9th centuries. The development of the stirrup allowed these soldiers to fight effectively while remaining mounted, marking an important military innovation. This new form of warfare contributed to the establishment of the feudal system, which provided a degree of security in an age marked by chaos and marauding tribes following the fall of the Roman Empire.

Feudalism and Social Structure

Feudalism, which arose primarily in France, defined the hierarchical structure of society during the Middle Ages. Land ownership became the primary source of wealth, leading to a system in which nobles received land grants (fields) from the king in exchange for their military service. This feudal bond was central to the chivalric ethos, as it emphasized loyalty, courage, and duty, which would later become key components of chivalric ideals.

The rise of chivalry is therefore closely linked to the expansion of feudalism, the political and social system that dominated Europe between the 9th and 15th centuries. In this context, the knight, a mounted armed warrior, became the linchpin of feudal armies. In exchange for land or titles, these warriors swore loyalty to a feudal lord, offering protection and their prowess in battle. However, to consolidate their position in society, it was not enough to be an effective warrior. A code was needed that would distinguish the knight not only by his military ability, but also by his virtue, honor, and fidelity.

This code was shaped by a combination of Christian values, warrior ideals, and courtly norms. The Church played a crucial role in shaping the idea of chivalry. During the Middle Ages, the Church promoted the figure of the Christian knight, who should not only be brave on the battlefield, but also pious, fair, and a defender of the weak. Chivalry, in this sense, became a tool to civilize an often brutal and violent military class, giving them a moral mission beyond war.

Fundamental values of the chivalric code

The Code of Chivalry represents the moral and ethical guidelines followed by medieval knights, developed mainly between the 11th and 12th centuries. While its origins can be traced back to ancient traditions, the late medieval code emerged from a synthesis of Germanic and Roman martial practices that emphasized military bravery, service to others, and personal conduct.

Broadly speaking, the Code of Chivalry encompassed the rules and customs expected of knights, including virtues such as courtesy, generosity, courage, and nobility.

Chivalric ideals were based on a set of key values that formed the foundation of chivalry:

Loyalty: The knight was expected to be loyal to his lord, his king, and his land, as well as to the Church.

Treason was one of the worst crimes a knight could commit, as the code of honor that governed him depended on his ability to keep his word.

Courage and skill in combat: The knight was expected to be a skilled and brave warrior. The ability to fight on the battlefield was an essential requirement, and medieval tournaments helped knights demonstrate and hone these skills.

Generosity and protection of the weak: Chivalry was not just a military code. Knights were expected to use their strength to protect the defenseless, such as women, children, the elderly, and the poor. This ideal was closely linked to the Christian values of charity and service to the most vulnerable.

Courtesy and respect towards women: One of the most distinctive aspects of chivalry was its emphasis on respectful and courteous treatment of ladies. This courtly behavior was influenced by the tradition of courtly love, which idealized women as superior beings who should be revered and protected, in part, due to the Christian influence on the cult of the Virgin Mary. However, this concept was far from implying gender equality; rather, it reinforced the vision of women as objects of worship and protection within a patriarchal system.

It should be noted that the relationship between men and women, immersed in patriarchy, finds part of its reason in the fact that in the Middle Ages, the average life expectancy was around 35 years, with high infant mortality, so it was essential to protect the health of women and their children, in exchange for the man taking the risks of the external defense of the home and the kingdom. From this need to its extension to other sectors of life, it was only a matter of time.

Honor and justice: Justice and honor were fundamental principles that guided the actions of a knight. Honor was seen as a personal value, a reflection of one's integrity and righteousness. The chivalric code also dictated that knights should be fair in their dealings, both with allies and enemies.

The Influence of Courtly Love

The concept of courtly love, a literary and social phenomenon that emerged between the 11th and 13th centuries, primarily in the courts of France and Provence, idealized love and celebrated the emotional experiences of knights and noblewomen. Troubadours played an important role in this cultural phenomenon, composing poetry that extolled the virtues of noble and chaste love, often directed at unattainable figures.

The interweaving of these romantic narratives with tales of chivalry contributed to the evolution of the definition of chivalry, which emphasized not only martial prowess but also the moral and ethical standards expected of knights. As chivalry evolved, it became a complex set of ideals and practices, profoundly influencing medieval society and its cultural output, including literature, art, and the formation of chivalric orders, further solidifying its importance in European history.

Courtly love exalted an idealized relationship between a knight and a lady, in which the knight was driven to do great deeds to win the favor of his beloved. This love was often platonic and distant, and in many instances the lady was a married woman, giving it a forbidden and, at the same time, more romantic character.

Courtly love literature reinforced the notion that the knight should treat women with reverence and respect, an attitude that, while it could seem admiring, also consolidated power inequalities between men and women. Women, in the context of courtly love, were seen as unattainable muses whose function was to inspire virtue and heroic acts in knights, but their role was essentially passive.

Chivalry, Power, and Social Control

From a sociological perspective, chivalry can be interpreted as a form of social control. The chivalric code served to regulate the behavior of knights, ensuring that their military skills were not used uncontrollably, but rather channeled into the service of feudal lords and the Church. Through chivalry, the violence inherent to the warrior class was transformed into an instrument of power that, at the same time, asserted dominance over the most vulnerable sectors of society, such as peasants and women.

By imposing an ideal of protection and respect towards women, chivalry also reinforced gender hierarchies. While women were elevated in chivalric discourse, they were still seen as dependent beings who required the protection and guidance of men. In this way, chivalry helped to consolidate patriarchy, legitimizing a system in which men-maintained power over women, but under a veil of nobility and devotion.

Contemporary relevance

Despite the decline of the medieval knightly class, the principles of chivalry still resonate today, serving as ethical guidelines that encourage people to strive for honor and integrity in their personal and professional lives.

Concepts such as loyalty, justice, courage, and generosity remain central to modern ethics and interpersonal relationships and reflect an eternal aspiration to embody the virtues of the Code of Chivalry.

The birth of chivalry was a multifaceted process that responded to the need to organize and civilize the warrior class of medieval Europe. By combining Christian ideals, warrior values, and courtly norms, chivalry became a code of conduct that defined the behavior of noblemen for centuries. Although many of its practices and values have disappeared or been transformed, the essence of chivalry remains the subject of debate and reflection in contemporary discussions about gender, morality, and courtesy in human relations.

Chapter 2
Evolution of chivalry through the centuries

Chivalry, as it was conceived in the Middle Ages, has not remained static. Over the centuries, its meaning and manifestations have changed, adapting to social, political, and economic transformations. From its beginnings as a military code for the nobility, chivalry evolved into a series of values associated with masculine behavior, influenced by factors as diverse as Christianity, the Industrial Revolution, and the rise of feminist movements. In this chapter, we will explore how chivalry has changed from the Middle Ages to the present, and how these transformations reflect changes in power, gender, and class structures.

Medieval Chivalry: A Military and Christian Foundation

In its original form, chivalry was a code of conduct that regulated the behavior of medieval knights, focusing on loyalty, honor, and the defense of the weak, especially women and children. Its primary function was military and social: knights served their feudal lords and the Church, protecting their lands and the established order. However, the religious component added to the chivalric code not only moderated the violence inherent in the warrior class but also introduced elements of Christian morality, such as piety and charity.

As feudalism became more established, chivalry took on a more refined character, especially in European courts. Here the concept of "courtly love" emerged, which idealized the relationships between knights and ladies. The knight was not only a protector, but also a devoted servant of women, albeit in a context in which gender inequality was the norm. In this sense, medieval chivalry consolidated male power, while relegating women to an idealized but passive role.

Orders of Chivalry

Orders of chivalry emerged as formal institutions in the late medieval period, reflecting the ideals of chivalry through structured codes of conduct and mutual obligations between knights. One of the earliest examples is the Order of the Garter, founded by Edward III in 1348 to inspire nobles to fight in France. Members of this order were selected for their chivalrous virtues, including courage and loyalty, and took a solemn oath to uphold the statutes of the order.

Notable Orders

• The Order of the Star

Founded between 1350 and 1364, the Order of the Star aimed to promote chivalry and honor among its members. It included a controversial clause forbidding retreat in battle, which, while a noble principle, often led to disastrous outcomes, such as the significant losses during the Battle of Brittany in 1353.

- **The Order of the Golden Fleece**

The Order of the Golden Fleece, founded in Bruges by Philip the Good, Duke of Burgundy, was created to celebrate his marriage to Isabella of Portugal. This order still exists today. Philip defined twelve chivalric virtues for the order, including faith, justice, and courage, which were to guide his knights in their conduct.

Impact on military culture

The orders of chivalry played a crucial role in shaping the military ethos of their time, influencing both the battlefield and civilian life. By the late medieval period, the principles of chivalry had begun to be challenged by the realities of war, as evidenced by the Battle of Agincourt in 1415, where King Henry V ordered the execution of over 3,000 French prisoners, including knights. This action contradicted the code of chivalry and highlighted a departure from traditional chivalric ideals in military conduct.

Influence on later military organizations

The customs and structures established by the orders of chivalry laid the foundations for modern military organizations. The hierarchy and codes of conduct observed by these medieval orders can still be seen in contemporary elite military units, which are often considered a form of modern nobility among the armed forces.

Chivalry in Literature

Chivalric literature encompasses a rich genre that celebrates the ideals and values of chivalry, including bravery, honor, and courtly love. Originating in the medieval period, this genre reflects cultural changes during the transition from oral to written traditions, in which narratives featuring knights, quests, and moral dilemmas took center stage.

Development of Chivalric Themes

By the late Middle Ages, illuminated manuscripts had played a major role in establishing chivalric values that permeated aristocratic culture and influenced social norms and ideals.

The literary cycles known as the Matter of France and the Matter of Britain, particularly the tales surrounding King Arthur and his knights, popularized chivalric themes and set a framework for later literary works.

Characteristics of Chivalric Romance

Chivalric novels typically focus on heroic protagonists embarking on dangerous quests, illustrating themes such as courtly love and the pursuit of honor. These narratives display intricate character development and narrative structures that significantly influenced Middle English literature.

Many works, such as Sir Gawain and the Green Knight, Sir Thomas Malory's Le Morte d'Arthur, and the works of Ludovico Ariosto, highlight the romantic form and archetype of the hero's quest, serving as reflections of the ideals and aspirations of their time.

Influence and Legacy

The impact of chivalric literature extends beyond its immediate historical context, influencing later literary traditions and shaping modern perceptions of the medieval era. Authors such as Dante, Spenser, and Tennyson have drawn on chivalric themes, integrating them into the fabric of contemporary literature.

Despite having gone through periods of decline, such as in the early 17th century when Miguel de Cervantes parodied them in Don Quixote, the romantic tropes established by chivalric tales remain integral to the modern understanding of medieval culture, evoking images of knights, damsels in distress, and heroic adventures.

The romanticization of chivalry

The chivalric novel is a genre of medieval literature that epitomizes the ideals and adventures of knights, often intertwined with themes of romantic love, bravery, and the pursuit of honor. These narratives typically feature heroic protagonists who embark on dangerous quests, reflecting the values of chivalry that prevailed in medieval society.

The tales are characterized by their intricate character development and complex narrative structures, marking a significant evolution in Middle English literature that influenced later literary works.

Evolution of the Chivalric Romance

The genre emerged as a distinctive form of narrative in the noble courts of the High Middle Ages and early modern Europe, initially written in languages such as Old French and later expanding to include English, Spanish, and Italian.

Early romances often focused on folkloric themes, including knights, mystical women, and magical creatures, and gradually shifted to highlight themes of courtly love and heroic journeys.

In the late medieval period, chivalric romances began to emphasize the interplay between love and chivalric conduct, interweaving romantic ideals with the moral codes expected of knights.

This evolution was marked by a shift from epic tales focused solely on military valor to narratives that celebrated personal honor, loyalty, and the ennobling power of love.

Notable Works and Authors

Important works in the chivalric romance genre include Sir Gawain and the Green Knight, which combines elements of Arthurian legend with moral complexity, and the influential texts of Chrétien de Troyes, which introduced nuanced characterizations and an emphasis on courtly love.

The writings of Geoffroi de Charny, particularly his Book of Chivalry, further articulated the virtues and priorities of chivalry during the 14th century, emphasizing the importance of martial skill and noble conduct.

Impact on Literature and Culture

Chivalric romances played a crucial role in shaping medieval literature and popular culture, serving as models for later literary works and continuing to influence narratives today. Romanticized ideals of chivalry, encompassing honor, loyalty, and the pursuit of romantic fulfillment, are deeply embedded in the collective imagination of the medieval period and beyond, highlighting the legacy of this literary genre.

Decline of Chivalry

Chivalry, once an important code of conduct for medieval knights, began to experience a notable decline during the late medieval period. This decline can be attributed to several interrelated factors.

One of the most important reasons for the decline of chivalry was the changing nature of warfare. As firearms gained prominence on the battlefield, traditional virtues and combat skills associated with the knightly class lost relevance. The rise of gunpowder weapons changed military strategies, diminishing the importance of heavily armored cavalry and the ideals of personal valor that chivalry celebrated.

The Transition to the Renaissance: Cultural and Social Changes

The emergence of a merchant middle class further eroded the feudal social structure that had supported chivalry. As cities and towns grew, merchants and artisans gained wealth and influence, challenging the traditional aristocracy. This economic shift reduced the relevance of chivalric ideals, which were closely tied to the noble class and its values.

• Growing Cynicism and Disillusionment
The late medieval period was characterized by growing cynicism and disillusionment regarding the idealized vision of chivalry and courtly love depicted in literature. This disconnects with everyday realities led to a questioning of the values espoused by chivalric literature. The once-celebrated ideals of honor, loyalty, and service began to be seen as outdated, giving way to a more selfish approach to life.

• Literature and criticism
Despite a revival of chivalric literature in the late 15th century, criticism arose about the decline of true chivalric values. William Worcester (English chronicler and antiquarian), for example, criticized the nobility in the late 15th century, suggesting that genuine chivalry was a relic of the past and no longer reflected contemporary realities.

Literature celebrating chivalry was often contrasted with works that portrayed it as increasingly disconnected from the values and behaviors of the time.

Legacy of Chivalry

With the decline of the feudal system in the 15th century and the rise of the Renaissance, the role of knights began to change. Medieval wars, which had dominated the lives of knights, were replaced by mercenary armies and more organized systems of state warfare. Therefore, the concept of chivalry lost its strict military relevance, but it did not disappear. In fact, during the Renaissance, chivalry was transformed into an ideal of courtly behavior that integrated skills such as diplomacy, cultural refinement, and civilized behavior.

The figure of the "knight" in this era was more associated with nobility and courtesy than with war. Novels of chivalry, such as those written by Miguel de Cervantes, satirized the obsolescence of medieval chivalry, reflecting the distance between the idealized image of the knight and the social reality of the time. However, the chivalric ideal persisted as a model of masculine virtue, increasingly focused on social etiquette and civilized interactions rather than warfare or physical defense.

Ultimately, while the core principles of chivalry (such as loyalty, honor, and duty) continued to influence modern military culture, the social context in which chivalry thrived had changed irrevocably. The codes of conduct that once defined knights were transformed into new interpretations, often disconnected from their original meanings, that reflected evolving values and social norms.

Enlightenment and the Transformation of Chivalry

The 18th century, with the Enlightenment, marked another turn in the evolution of chivalry. The ideals of equality and rationality promoted by Enlightenment thinkers challenged feudal hierarchies and the values associated with nobility. However, chivalry did not disappear but was reinterpreted. Upper-class men still adhered to a code of conduct that emphasized courtesy, but this code was now more universal, applying to the propertied classes in general and not just military gentlemen.

During this period, chivalry also began to emphasize men's moral responsibilities toward women and children. Rather than simply protecting them, men were expected to treat them fairly and with respect, reflecting the shift toward a more orderly and "civilized" society. However, these responsibilities were still based on gender power inequality. The man was still seen as the protector and authority figure, while the woman remained in a dependent role.

The Victorian Era: Morality and Chivalry

Chivalry underwent another significant change during the Victorian era of the 19th century. The Industrial Revolution transformed social structures, and the new middle class adopted the chivalric ideals of nobility, reinterpreting them to fit the strict moral standards of the time. During this time, chivalry was centered on morality and self-control. Victorian men were expected to be honorable, discreet, and above all, protective of "female virtue."

The concept of the "separate sphere" was key to the Victorian view of chivalry. Women were seen as morally superior, but at the same time vulnerable, beings whose purity had to be safeguarded by men. This idea reinforced gender hierarchies, even though, in some cases, women were beginning to have greater visibility in the public sphere.

Again, we find some logic in this supposed female disadvantage or submission. At a time when contraception did not exist, it was necessary to protect women from unwanted pregnancies and to preserve them for those who felt true affection for them, who, in the event of pregnancy, would not abandon them, and would stay to protect them and their child. This need became the "virtue" that women were expected to preserve. On the other hand, the candidate had to offer not only affection but also prove that he was worth selecting as a partner. In that sense, if the man brought with him a history of female conquests, it meant that others had desired him, so this man stood out among others.

20th Century: The Crisis and Reinvention of Chivalry

The 20th century brought devastating wars, the expansion of civil rights, and the rise of feminist movements, all of which profoundly challenged the traditional ideal of chivalry. The World Wars dismantled many of the social hierarchies of the past, and men could no longer claim their place as exclusive protectors, as women played fundamental roles in industry, the economy, and the war effort.

In addition, feminist movements in the 20th century began to question the patriarchal foundation of chivalry. Women no longer wanted to be seen as fragile or dependent on male protection. Chivalrous principles, such as opening the door for a woman or paying the bill on a date, were seen by many as paternalistic gestures that reinforced gender inequality. Throughout the 20th century, chivalry faced a crisis, as the social norms that supported it began to break down.

However, it did not disappear altogether. Instead, chivalry was reinterpreted in some contexts as a form of mutual respect and courtesy between genders. Ideals of protection and devotion to women gave way in favor of more genuine equality, although certain chivalrous gestures persisted as part of expected social behavior.

Traditional chivalrous gestures by men toward women:

• Opening the door for the woman to go first.

• Giving up your seat on public transportation or in crowded spaces.
• Helping to carry heavy objects or shopping bags.
• Offering your coat when the woman is cold.
• Walking on the side of the street to protect the woman from traffic.
• Offering your arms when walking together, especially in formal situations.
• Paying the bill on a date or outing.
• Helping her sit down by moving her chair in restaurants or events.
• Waiting for the woman to start eating before starting your meal.
• Opening the car door and helping the woman get in or out of the vehicle.
• Protect her in the rain by offering an umbrella or covering her with your coat.
• Complimenting her appearance or personality with respect and courtesy.
• Yielding the right of way when entering or leaving a place.
• Sending flowers or small gifts for no special reason, as a gesture of appreciation.
• Offering your hand to help the woman up or down stairs or difficult terrain.

These gestures, although valued in their time, are today being reinterpreted in the context of egalitarian relationships.

21st Century: Chivalry in the Age of Feminism and Woke

In the 21st century, chivalry has been left on shaky ground. While some see it as an anachronism that reinforces patriarchy, others argue that it can be reinterpreted as a set of standards of mutual respect and consideration between the genders. In the era of feminist movements and the rise of the Woke movement, traditional chivalry has been harshly criticized for its involvement in perpetuating unequal power relations.

The contemporary challenge lies in finding a balance between courtesy and equality. The idea that men should protect or act in a special way towards women is no longer compatible with gender equality values. However, the values of respect, empathy, and consideration can survive if they are redefined within an equitable relationship free of gender hierarchies.

Chivalry has come a long way from its origins in feudal Europe to the present day. It has evolved from a military code to a set of courtly and moral norms, but its evolution has always been marked by hierarchies of power, class, and gender. In the 21st century, chivalry remains a subject of debate, and its future depends on how it adapts to the demands of a society that increasingly values equality and mutual respect among all individuals.

Chapter 3
Chivalry in modern society:
A vestige in decline

Chivalry, once the mainstay of social interaction and male behavior, has undergone a profound transformation over the centuries. In modern society, many view chivalry as a vestige of the past, a relic of a time when social norms and power structures were different than they are today. The concept of chivalry has been revisited and questioned as gender roles have changed and equal rights movements have gained ground. In this chapter, we will explore how chivalry has declined in modern society from a historical and sociological perspective, and what factors have contributed to its apparent demise.

Chivalry in Transition: From Nobility to the Middle Class

For centuries, chivalry was a code of conduct exclusive to nobility, associated primarily with medieval knights. Over time, however, its core values—such as respect, protection of the weak, and courtesy toward women—were adopted by the middle class, especially during the Victorian era. The Industrial Revolution and the social changes it brought about contributed to the expansion of these ideals, as the emerging classes saw chivalry as a model of masculine behavior that served to preserve social and moral order.

However, as the 20th century progressed, the social and economic context changed dramatically. Growing social mobility, increased civil rights, and the rise of feminist movements began to challenge the structures that supported chivalry. Gender equality began to gain ground, and with it, the idea that men should act as protectors and guardians of women was questioned. The role of the chivalrous man, which traditionally involved being a "protector" in a hierarchical relationship, began to be seen as a paternalistic and unnecessary gesture.

The influence of feminism and the redefinition of gender roles

One of the main factors that contributed to the decline of chivalry in modern society was the impact of feminism. Since the second half of the 20th century, feminist movements have challenged traditional gender norms that upheld the idea that men should behave protectively and condescendingly towards women. It was argued that chivalry, far from being a sign of respect, perpetuated the idea that women were weaker or incapable of taking care of themselves, which kept them in a subordinate role in society.

Feminism, in its fight for equal rights and opportunities, promoted the idea that women did not need the protection of men, but should have equal opportunities to make decisions, work and live independently. In this context, chivalrous gestures, such as opening a door for a woman or paying the bill at a dinner party, began to be perceived by some as actions that reinforced an unequal power dynamic.

Equality demanded a more balanced relationship, in which traditional gender roles were overcome.

Masculinity

The concept of masculinity has been a topic of debate for centuries, but in recent decades, it has become more evident with the emergence of different categorizations that attempt to define the types of men and their roles in society. Among these concepts, the categories of "alpha male", "beta", "sigma" and other classifications that have emerged in online discussions and social spaces stand out. These labels have captured the popular imagination but have also sparked criticism and controversy as they simplify and stereotype what it means to be a man. Below, we will address the origin of these categories, what they represent, and their impact on the way men see themselves and others.

• The "Alpha Male"

The term "alpha male" comes from the study of animal behavior, particularly species such as wolves, in which pack leaders are dominant and control other members of the group. In human society, the "alpha" has become synonymous with a man who is strong, assertive, successful, and socially dominant. This type of man is presented as the natural leader, the one who imposes his will, attracts the attention of women and is successful both in the workplace and in his personal life.

In popular cultures and certain self-help and masculinity circles, the alpha is idealized as the man everyone should aspire to be. Attributes such as self-confidence, competitiveness, and emotional control are presented as essential for an "alpha male." However, this figure can also be associated with attitudes of machismo and excessive dominance, which can reinforce stereotypes of a rigid and toxic masculinity that excludes any form of vulnerability or empathy.

• The "Beta Male"

In contrast to the alpha, the "beta male" is the man who, according to stereotypes, lacks the dominant and aggressive characteristics that define the alpha. He is portrayed as someone more passive, reserved, and emotionally open, which often places him in a position of subordination, both socially and romantically.

The term "beta" has been used pejoratively in many online spaces, especially in the Manosphere (the set of male online communities that discuss topics such as gender relations and masculinity). Betas are often portrayed as men who are incapable of leading or competing, being relegated to the background, both in the workplace and in romantic relationships.

However, this simplified categorization ignores that many qualities associated with the "beta," such as empathy, cooperation, and sensitivity, are important and beneficial assets in many situations. Being a "beta" does not necessarily imply a lack of worth or success, but popular culture often perpetuates the idea that being a beta is a negative thing.

• The "Sigma Male"

More recently, the concept of the "sigma male" has gained popularity, describing a man who possesses the qualities of an alpha, but who chooses not to follow established societal norms of leadership and dominance. He is often described as a "lone wolf," someone who does not seek recognition or power within a group, but who nonetheless possesses a high level of confidence and personal success.

The sigma is seen as independent, self-sufficient, and detached from societal expectations. Unlike the alpha, who leads and seeks external validation, sigma is not concerned with status and prefers to operate outside the social structure. This figure is attractive to those men who do not identify with the traditional leadership role of the alpha, but who also do not wish to be perceived as betas or subordinates.

The Sigma male is in many ways a response to the increasing diversity of male role models recognized in contemporary society. Despite his advantages in terms of independence and self-sufficiency, he has also been criticized for idealizing a solitary and aloof lifestyle, which can foster emotional isolation.

• The Gamma Male

The gamma male is seen as intelligent, but lacking in developed social skills. He is often perceived as resentful of hierarchical structures that favor alphas and sigmas. He is often associated with introversion and a lack of social interaction skills.

• **The Delta Male**

Delta men are often described as ordinary workers, without the charisma or ambition of alphas or sigmas. They have a functional role in society but do not seek leadership or excel excessively in interpersonal relationships.

• **The Omega**

At the opposite end of the spectrum is the omega, who is portrayed as the marginalized individual, both socially and romantically. This stereotype is used to describe men who are unsuccessful in either their professional or personal lives, and who are seen as the "losers" within the male hierarchy.

Criticism of the Alpha, Beta, and Sigma Categories

These categorizations of masculinity have come under heavy criticism, as they simplify and reinforce rigid stereotypes about what it means to be a man. While some may find value in identifying with one of these labels, critics argue that this categorization framework fails to consider the complexity and diversity of human experience.

<u>Simplification of male identity</u>: Men cannot be reduced to a single category of alpha, beta, or sigma. Each person's identity is made up of a mix of characteristics and traits that go beyond aggressiveness or passivity, leadership, or submission.

<u>Reinforcement of traditional gender roles</u>: The categories tend to perpetuate stereotypes of traditional masculinity, in which a man must be strong, and

dominant, and avoid showing emotion. This is not only limiting but also contributes to a toxic view of masculinity that can negatively affect men's mental health.

<u>Emotional Disconnection:</u> The pressure to fit into one of these labels can lead men to disconnect from their emotions and their relationships. By emphasizing power, dominance, or independence, these categorizations can encourage a type of behavior that excludes vulnerability, empathy, and authenticity.

Evolving Masculinity

As we move toward a broader and more diverse understanding of what it means to be a man, it is crucial to question and rethink narratives that promote rigid categorizations of masculinity. Rather than pigeonholing men in terms of "alpha" or "beta," it is more productive to recognize that masculinity can and should be a multifaceted experience. Men can be leaders and still show emotional vulnerability, be independent without being isolated, and be strong without silencing their feelings.

Masculinity in the 21st century must reflect the complexity and diversity of human experiences, where men can define their roles and behaviors without relying on limiting stereotypes. The categories of alpha, beta, sigma, and more may be helpful to some in their search for identity, but they should not be the only models to follow. Ultimately, the challenge is to create a space where all men, regardless of style or approach, can thrive, express themselves freely, and build healthy, balanced relationships.

Changes in modern masculinity

The redefinition of chivalry in modern society is also linked to changes in the perception of masculinity. The concept of masculinity has historically been associated with strength, protection, and leadership—all values present in traditional chivalry. However, societal expectations about what it means to be a "man" have radically changed in recent decades.

Today, masculinity is understood in more diverse and flexible ways, which has affected the way men relate to women and other men. Rather than feeling compelled to play a protective or dominant role, many men are more comfortable embracing a form of masculinity that emphasizes empathy and equality. This shift has made chivalry, in its most traditional form, less relevant, as men no longer feel the same pressure to act as women's "guardians."

In addition, the rise of movements such as the "new man" and initiatives on men's mental health have fostered a form of masculinity that challenges traditional stereotypes. The modern man is increasingly aware of the need for more equitable relationships that are less based on pre-established gender roles.

The Impact of the Woke Movement and the Questioning of Traditions

The Woke movement, which emerged in the 21st century as a purported response to social injustices and inequality, has also played a role in the decline of chivalry. This movement has promoted the idea of complete gender equality and has questioned norms and traditions that perpetuate any form of oppression or inequality, including chivalrous gestures that imply a distinction of power between men and women.

Within the framework of this movement, chivalry has been criticized for being a remnant of patriarchy and machismo, a system in which men occupied a position of power over women. As modern societies strive to be more inclusive and equitable, traditions that reinforce gender stereotypes are increasingly seen as problematic. The woke movement has prompted a re-evaluation of how we interact socially, and chivalry, as it was known in the past, has not escaped this critical review.

Chivalry in the Digital Age

Another important factor in the decline of chivalry is the impact of the digital age and the transformation of social relationships. Online interactions, through social media and dating apps, have dramatically changed the way people relate and communicate. In this context, traditional social codes, including chivalrous gestures, have lost relevance.

The immediacy and impersonality of many digital interactions have reduced the need or space for the expression of traditional courtesies. Furthermore, online anonymity has fostered a culture where respect and courtesy are often relegated, and where human interaction is, in many cases, more pragmatic than emotional.

A declining vestige or a transformation?

Despite these changes, chivalry has not disappeared entirely. In some contexts, it is still valued as a form of courtesy and mutual respect, even if it has lost its sense of "protection" that characterized it in the past. Today, some see chivalry as an opportunity to promote respect and empathy, if it is detached from gender hierarchies.

The question that remains is whether chivalry is in decline because it no longer has a place in modern society, or whether it is simply in the process of transforming into something new. In a society that increasingly values equality, can chivalry adapt and continue to be relevant? Or, on the contrary, are we witnessing the disappearance of a vestige of a time when gender roles were clearly defined?

Chapter 4
Feminism and the redefinition of modern man

Feminism has been one of the most influential forces in the social and cultural transformation of the 20th and 21st centuries, profoundly altering gender norms, social relations, and especially the perception of masculinity. As women have fought for and made progress toward equal rights and opportunities, men have also experienced a redefinition of their identity, roles, and place in society. This chapter examines how feminism has prompted a revision of what it means to be a "modern man" from a historical and sociological perspective, and how this evolution is affecting the dynamics of power, gender, and interpersonal relationships.

The emergence of feminism: Challenging traditional gender norms

Feminism as a social movement has gone through several waves that have redefined its goals and areas of focus. The first wave, during the 19th and early 20th centuries, focused on civil and political rights, such as women's suffrage. The second wave, which began in the 1960s and 1970s, addressed not only legal rights but also social norms that oppressed women in the domestic, workplace, and sexual realms. It was in this context that feminism began to directly challenge traditional constructions of masculinity.

Gender norms that defined men as protectors, providers, and authority figures were questioned. Feminism criticized the idea that relationships between men and women should be based on power hierarchies and advocated a new way of interacting between the genders, based on equality and mutual respect. This critique not only destabilized constructions of femininity but also those of masculinity, by exposing that many of the expectations imposed on men were deeply linked to systems of gender oppression.

Second-Wave Feminism and the Questioning of Masculinity

With the second wave of feminism, a deeper analysis emerged of how patriarchy not only affected women but also men. Feminists of this era stressed that the patriarchal system, by imposing rigid gender norms, also limited men's emotional expression and life choices. Ideals of masculinity, based on strength, control, material success, and lack of vulnerability, created unsustainable pressure for many men, who felt they had to conform to these norms to be socially accepted.

This questioning gave rise to the concept of "toxic masculinity," a term that refers to men's behaviors and attitudes that are harmful to themselves and others. Toxic masculinity includes characteristics such as emotional repression, aggression, dominance over others, and avoidance of anything considered "feminine." As feminism critiqued these norms, a space began to emerge for a redefinition of what it meant to be a man, one in which empathy, vulnerability, and gender equality could be central parts of male identity.

Third-wave Feminism and Intersectionality

Third-wave feminism, beginning in the 1990s, further broadened the movement's focus, focusing on intersectionality, that is, how experiences of oppression are not only based on gender, but also on race, class, sexuality, and other factors. In this context, the redefinition of the modern man was not only influenced by feminism, but also by other social movements that advocated for the rights of racial minorities, LGBTQ+ people, and other marginalized groups.

Men also began to experience greater diversity in their models of masculinity. There was no longer one acceptable way to be a man. Social activism promoted greater acceptance of diverse male identities, such as QUEER men, men of color, and those who rejected traditional gender roles. This shift reflected the impact of feminist struggles and the understanding that systems of oppression affected all people, regardless of their gender.

The Modern Man and the Break with Patriarchy

Throughout the 21st century, feminism has continued to push for an overhaul of masculine norms. Campaigns and movements, such as "HeForShe" and "MenEngage," have highlighted that the fight for gender equality is not only a responsibility of women but also of men. These movements have highlighted how patriarchy oppresses both genders and how men can play an active role in dismantling the structures that perpetuate inequality.

The modern man is torn between being increasingly willing to question patriarchy and his gender expectations, and his tradition as a gentleman. There has been a greater acceptance of emotional vulnerability, a rejection of violence, and a search for more equitable relationships, but at the same time, behaviors that women once appreciated have been lost. The notion that men should be the "providers" is being replaced by the idea that they can share economic, domestic, and emotional responsibilities with their partners, although many women are reluctant to lose their ancestral privileges in the female role. At the same time, men are adopting more active fatherhood, participating more in child-rearing, and redefining the role of the father as someone who is also a caregiver and emotionally present.

Machismo in society: An obstacle to equality

Machismo is an ideology that promotes the superiority of men over women, perpetuating gender stereotypes that limit the opportunities and rights of both sexes. Although machismo primarily affects women by imposing traditional roles that subordinate them in the home, work, and public life, it also harms men by imposing rigid expectations on them about what it means to be "masculine." This system reinforces the idea that men must be dominant, aggressive, and emotionally unattainable, which makes it difficult to build relationships.

In many aspects of society, sexism is still present. In the workplace, women continue to face wage inequalities and obstacles to accessing positions of power. In everyday life, there is daily harassment, sexist comments, and the reflection of a normalization of gender violence, which has roots in this mentality.

To eradicate sexism in society, it is essential to recognize that it is not just about individual behavior, but a structural problem deeply rooted in our institutions and culture. From the media to the laws, the influence of sexism manifests itself in practices that reinforce inequality. For example, the portrayal of women in television and film often reduces them to secondary roles or objectifies them, while men are portrayed as heroes or leaders, perpetuating

It is important for men to actively engage in the fight against machismo, questioning their behaviors and attitudes, and challenging the social environment that reinforces these ideas. Change will not be achieved solely through public policies or legal changes, although these are essential. It also requires a personal and collective effort to transform social norms and educate future generations about gender equity.

Gender equality benefits not only women but society. A society that values and respects the contributions and capabilities of all its members, regardless of their gender, is a more just, creative, and productive society. Overcoming machismo brings us closer to that ideal, where equity, respect, and cooperation replace oppression and competition based on traditional gender roles.

Criticisms of "Gender Equality": The Complexity of Recognizing Differences

Although gender equality is a widely promoted ideal, it has been criticized by some sectors who argue that it does not consider the obvious biological, psychological, and social differences between men and women. These critics point out that trying to impose absolute equality can lead to ignoring fundamental aspects of human beings.

One of the key points of these criticisms is that men and women, in general, have different physical, hormonal, and behavioral characteristics that influence their interests, abilities, and preferences. For example, some argue that equality policies that seek parity in all fields, such as in the workplace or education, ignore that there may be natural differences in the inclination towards certain professions or lifestyles. From this perspective, trying to equalize results between genders, such as having a 50/50 distribution in all professions or roles, could force men and women to perform roles to which they are not innately attracted.

For example, in areas such as education or work, some suggest that equality policies that seek an equitable distribution of gender across all professions might be ignoring the reality that men and women, on average, have different inclinations towards certain types of jobs. Professions such as engineering or nursing, which have typically been dominated by one or the other gender, are often at the center of these debates. The criticism here is not based on maintaining traditional roles, but on respecting that career choices can be influenced by biological factors and not necessarily by gender barriers imposed by the prevailing culture.

Critics also point out that, in the fight for equality, some problems affecting men have been neglected, such as high mortality rates in dangerous jobs, mental health problems, or the fact that they often receive harsher sentences for the same crimes as women. In addition, in many countries, men face disadvantages in child custody disputes or in court systems where laws favor women in cases of domestic violence, fuelling the perception that the equality promoted is not truly equitable.

These critiques do not seek to delegitimize gender equality, but rather to promote a more nuanced approach that recognizes both differences and similarities between genders. Rather than seeking forced parity in all aspects, it proposes that the diversity of capabilities and aspirations between men and women be respected, allowing each gender to reach its potential without the pressure of meeting predefined quotas or standards.

The challenge of gender equality, according to this view, is not to eliminate differences, but to build a social and legal framework that allows both men and women to have equal opportunities to develop based on their talents, desires, and characteristics. Ultimately, true equality must adapt to natural realities and promote mutual respect that allows each individual to flourish according to their circumstances.

Another school of critics claims that feminism did not prosper as a "defense of women's rights" but rather because of a plot created by 19th-century capitalism. If we look at the standard of living in the mid-20th century, a typical family consisted of a father who worked outside the home and a mother who took care of the house and the children. Few women worked. The husband's earnings were enough for a full life, acquiring a house and car in a short time. Children grew up under the protection of their present mother. According to this school of thought, capitalists, to increase their profits, needed to produce more, and to do so they required more labor, setting their sights on women who were housewives. This is how the feminist movement evolved from its objectives of obtaining the female vote and greater freedoms to ruthlessly fighting men. The new discourse contained ideas of "patriarchy" and "macho world" that plunged women into the "home" and that the best and most interesting things were in the man's world (12 hours away from home, putting up with the bad mood of the bosses and bearing the responsibility of ensuring that their family did not lack anything), that it was okay to hire a daycare center to raise a child, instead of doing it herself; and that junk food was the same as home-cooked food.

This is how women left the home to look for work, causing the labor market to become saturated and salaries to fall due to an excess of supply, meaning that today a single income is not enough, and both men must work to obtain the basics, because even a humble house cannot be achieved alone.

Masculinity in crisis: Resistance and Acceptance

Despite the advances, not all men have accepted the redefinition of masculinity promoted by feminism. For some, social changes have generated an identity crisis. Movements such as "Men's Rights Activists" have emerged in response to the perception that feminism has "displaced" men, putting forward a discourse that suggests men have lost power and status due to increasing gender equality.

This resistance reflects a discomfort at the disappearance of the "historical privileges" that men have enjoyed. However, it also highlights the difficulties some men face in adapting to a new social order in which they are no longer expected to be dominant or controlling. These men may experience insecurity or alienation, feeling that they have no clear place in a society that promotes equality and fairness.

On the other hand, a significant portion of the male population has embraced the change, recognizing that gender equality benefits everyone. Men who align themselves with feminist values see themselves as allies in the fight for a more just society and find new ways to express their masculinity in a more balanced and respectful way towards women and other men.

Consent culture and modern relationships

Another key aspect of the redefinition of the modern man is consent culture, which has gained prominence in recent decades. Feminism has advocated for relationships based on mutual consent and respect, which has transformed expectations around power dynamics in sexual and emotional relationships. In the past, gender norms often dictated that men take the initiative and decisions in relationships, while women were to be receptive or passive.

However, feminism has promoted the idea that relationships should be based on open communication and enthusiastic consent from all parties involved. This has challenged traditional power dynamics and prompted a re-evaluation of how men approach romantic and sexual relationships. The redefinition of the modern man involves, in this sense, greater responsibility in the way they interact in relationships and a rejection of dominating or controlling behaviors.

Feminism has played a pivotal role in transforming masculinity in modern society. From challenging traditional gender norms to promoting greater equality and mutual respect, feminism has pushed men to reflect on their place in the world and how they can contribute to a more just society. The redefinition of the modern man has not been a simple or uniform process. It has generated both acceptance and resistance, but it has opened new possibilities for men to be more authentic, vulnerable, and, above all, egalitarian.

Chapter 5
The Woke Movement:
Dismantling traditional codes

The rise of the woke movement has represented one of the most relevant social phenomena of the 21st century, promoting a profound re-evaluation of power structures, gender norms, racial relations, and traditional social codes. From its perspective, the woke movement seeks to dismantle the systems of oppression that have prevailed for centuries, addressing issues such as racial and gender inequality, sexual discrimination, and the impact of capitalism on people's lives. This chapter explores how the woke movement has redefined social discourses, gender roles, and traditional behavioral codes, focusing on its impact on contemporary society.

Origin and meaning of the woke movement

The term woke, which originally translates as "awake," has its roots in the African American civil rights movements in the United States. Initially, it was a warning to "wake up" to the racial injustices and systemic oppressions affecting black communities. Beginning in the 2010s, woke began to expand as a more general term encompassing a wide range of social and justice issues, including feminism, LGBTQ+ rights, climate justice, and critiques of capitalism.

The woke movement has been characterized by its focus on intersectionality—that is, how different systems of oppression (such as racism, sexism, and homophobia) intersect and affect people simultaneously. Through this lens, woke challenges established social norms and seeks to redesign a more equitable society, where historical and structural inequalities are dismantled.

Questioning tradition: The dismantling of traditional codes

One of the most radical aspects of the woke movement is its emphasis on the need to dismantle traditional codes that have governed social conduct and power relations. These codes include patriarchal norms, hierarchical structures of race and class, and ideas of binary gender, which have formed the basis of Western society for centuries. Woke challenges these established values, arguing that they have been historically used to perpetuate the oppression and marginalization of diverse groups.

For example, patriarchy, which has dominated gender relations throughout history, has been one of the institutions most challenged by the woke movement. Patriarchal norms not only limit women but also negatively affect men by imposing rigid roles and dominating behaviors on them. Woke advocates for a dissolution of these expectations, promoting freedom of gender expression and respect for the diversity of identities. In this sense, feminism and woke have intertwined in their fight for equality and the deconstruction of power structures that are perpetuated in traditional codes.

Impact on masculinity and gender roles

One of the biggest challenges presented by the woke movement is its impact on traditional concepts of masculinity. For centuries, social codes set clear expectations for men: to be protectors, providers, and authority figures. These ideas of masculinity were deeply tied to the idea of control and power, both over women and society at large.

However, woke has reframed masculinity, proposing a new framework based on vulnerability, empathy, and equality. The movement rejects the ideals of "toxic masculinity," which promote aggression, competition, and emotional repression as masculine values, and instead encourages greater flexibility in gender expression. This has led to a redefinition of male roles in modern society, where men are no longer forced to conform to the rigid patterns of behavior established by previous generations.

Woke also advocates for greater equity in relationships, where men and women share responsibilities equally. Rather than men being seen as the sole protectors or providers, the movement promotes relationships based on mutual consent, cooperation, and respect. This shift in expectations has created increased pressure for men to reconsider their role in society, adapting to a context in which traditional gender norms are in decline.

Intersectionality and Dismantling Structural Oppression

One of the most influential aspects of the Woke movement is its focus on intersectionality, a concept developed by feminist theorist Kimberlé Crenshaw in the 1980s. Intersectionality suggests that people do not experience oppression in isolation, but that various forms of discrimination (gender, race, class, sexuality, etc.) interrelate to create a unique experience of marginalization.

The woke movement uses this intersectional perspective to dismantle not only traditional gender and race codes, but also systems of economic, political, and social oppression. By recognizing the complexity of human identities, woke seeks to create a world in which all forms of inequality are challenged and eventually eliminated. In this sense, the woke movement not only aims to dismantle visible power structures but also the microaggressions and implicit biases that reinforce these inequalities in everyday life.

Cancel culture and its effects

One of the most controversial elements of the woke movement is cancel culture, a practice in which individuals or public figures are "canceled" or boycotted due to behavior or comments perceived as offensive or morally wrong. This practice has sparked intense debates about freedom of expression, social justice, and the limits of accountability in the public sphere.

Proponents of cancel culture argue that it is a necessary tool to hold accountable those who perpetuate racism, sexism, or any other form of oppression. At the same time, critics argue that this approach can be overly punitive, leading to disproportionate consequences such as loss of employment opportunities or social exile for mistakes that could be seen as momentary or fixable.

From a sociological perspective, cancel culture reflects the growing sensitivity to social injustices in the digital age. However, it also highlights a tension between the correction of historical wrongs and the possibility of redemption. This phenomenon can be seen as an attempt by the woke movement to dismantle traditional codes of power, where public figures were largely immune to consequences for their inappropriate behavior.

The Impact on the Power Structure: From Institutions to Popular Culture

The woke movement has not only influenced interpersonal relationships but has also penetrated social institutions and popular culture. Businesses, media, and entertainment industries have responded to the movement's demands by adjusting their policies and products to reflect a greater commitment to social justice and inclusion.

In popular culture, representations of gender, race, and sexual orientation have changed dramatically in recent years. Traditional narratives of dominant male heroes and subordinate women have been replaced by more diverse and inclusive stories that celebrate a variety of identities and experiences. This evolution in cultural representations is part of the process of dismantling traditional codes promoted by the woke movement, which seeks to make visible and give voice to those who have historically been marginalized.

At an institutional level, the woke movement has driven reforms in areas such as criminal justice, education, and labor policy. Calls for greater diversity, equity, and inclusion in the workplace have led to the implementation of awareness programs about implicit bias and systemic racism. Woke activism has also influenced hiring policies, seeking to reduce gender and racial disparities in sectors historically dominated by white men.

Criticism of the Woke Movement

Although the Woke movement has gained traction in recent years, it has also been subject to criticism, especially from conservative and traditionalist quarters. Critics argue that Woke encourages a "victimhood culture," in which people focus too much on past and present oppressions rather than promoting merit and individuality. In addition, some argue that Woke may further polarize society, creating a divide between the "woke" and those who resist social change.

Another point of criticism is the perception that the woke movement may fall into "moralism" - that is, the imposition of rigid ethical standards that do not allow for debate or dissent. For some, this may stifle freedom of expression and pluralism, fundamental values in a democracy. However, woke advocates argue that these changes are necessary to correct centuries of inequality and oppression, and that criticism often comes from those who benefit from the status quo.

The woke movement and the gentlemen

The woke movement has generated intense debate about many aspects of society, and one of the most discussed is how masculinity is understood and the traditional role of the man as a "gentleman". This movement, which places a strong emphasis on social justice, gender equity, and the fight against forms of oppression and discrimination, has critically reexamined many traditional gender roles, questioning their relevance and impact on current social dynamics.

The Woke Movement's View of Masculinity

For Woke, traditional masculinity, also known as "hegemonic masculinity," is largely tied to the perpetuation of patriarchal structures that favor male dominance and keep women and other marginalized groups in subordinate positions. This type of masculinity has historically been seen as aggressive, emotionally distant, dominant, and focused on control and power. In the context of Woke, this view is criticized for being limiting for both men and women.

From a Woke perspective, the problem with traditional masculinity is that it perpetuates stereotypes that not only reinforce gender inequality but also create harmful expectations for men themselves. Traditional notions that men should be the providers, protectors, and strong leaders tend to exclude emotional vulnerability and empathy, which can lead to toxic behaviors, such as emotional repression, aggression, and a lack of connection to one's own and other's emotions.

In this context, woke proposes a new masculinity, one in which men break free from these stereotypes and adopt more inclusive and equitable behaviors. Rather than focusing on dominance or one-sided protection, woke men focus on equality, emotional reciprocity, and respect for the boundaries and desires of others. Vulnerability and emotional openness are promoted, and expectations that men must be tough, invulnerable, and always in control are challenged.

The role of the gentleman under the woke lens

The concept of traditional chivalry has also been the subject of analysis within the woke movement. Behaviors that have historically been considered chivalrous—such as opening the door for a woman, paying her bill, or physically protecting her—are often interpreted as part of a patriarchal system that reinforces the idea that women are fragile, dependent, and in need of being protected or cared for by men. From this perspective, chivalry can be seen as a form of paternalism disguised as courtesy.

The problem, according to Woke, is that these gestures, while they may seem innocent or even generous, are often rooted in the idea that men should be the protectors and women the protected, perpetuating an unequal power dynamic. By constantly offering protection or assistance, the traditional chivalrous man may inadvertently be reinforcing the notion that women are not capable of taking care of themselves or that they need male guidance.

In this sense, woke promotes a reconfiguration of what it means to be "chivalrous" or respectful in relationships between men and women. Instead of polite gestures that reinforce gender differences and power roles, the movement proposes that respect and equality should be the guiding principles of any interaction. Politeness can be mutual and should not be based on assumptions about one gender's inability to do so over the other.

Criticisms of the woke approach to chivalry

However, not everyone agrees with Woke's interpretation of masculinity and chivalry. Some critics of the movement argue that by dismantling these gestures of courtesy, wokeness risks eliminating valuable aspects of human relationships. For some, chivalry is not necessarily an expression of power or control, but rather a way of expressing respect, consideration, and appreciation for others. From this perspective, the rejection of certain chivalrous gestures can be perceived as a denial of traditional forms of interaction that were once meaningful.

The argument is also made that differences between men and women should not be seen solely as a source of oppression, but as a reality that can be celebrated and respected without falling into machismo or sexism. For these critics, wokeness risks blurring the distinction between what can be a positive and negative gender dynamic, demonizing all displays of courtesy or protection simply because they are associated with traditional gender roles.

Masculinity and Chivalry in the Woke Future

Despite criticism, the woke movement has led to deep reflection on the impact of traditional masculinity and chivalry on power dynamics between the genders. The goal of Woke is not to eliminate politeness or respect in interactions between men and women but to promote a form of interaction that is free of the harmful stereotypes and stifling expectations that have traditionally accompanied these gestures.

The man in the woke context can still be respectful and considerate, but he will do so from a stance of equality, recognizing that his partner is not a "damsel in distress" in need of rescuing, but a human being with full agency and autonomy. Instead of chivalrous acts based on a perception of female weakness, woke men can show politeness in a way that celebrates equality and fosters more balanced relationships.

Finally, the woke movement has contributed to the expansion of what it means to be a man in the modern world. Challenging traditional notions of masculinity and chivalry has opened the door to new ways of being a man that is not tied to domination or protection but to collaboration, empathy, and mutual respect. In this sense, woke does not aim to destroy chivalry, but to reinvent it in a way that is aligned with contemporary values of equality and equity.

Men's movements

As a result of feminism and the woke movement, several social movements of men have emerged in response to these changes, some to redefine what it means to be a man in the contemporary world and others in the form of resistance or protest what they perceive as a threat to their rights or identities. Below we will discuss some of the more prominent men's social movements that have emerged in response:

• Men's Rights Movement
One of the most prominent movements in this category is the Men's Rights Movement (MRM). This movement originated in the 1970s and 1980s as a direct reaction to second-wave feminism. MRM activists argue that feminism has contributed to the marginalization of men in a variety of areas, including family law, access to child custody, reproductive rights, and representation in domestic violence issues.

MRM advocates claim that divorce and child custody laws tend to favor women, leaving many men without access to their children. They further argue that feminism has overshadowed the need to address specific issues facing men, such as high suicide rates, male dropouts, workplace discrimination, and a lack of resources for abused men.

While the MRM has addressed important issues, it has also been criticized by some of its more radical factions who adopt a misogynistic discourse, blaming women and feminism for all the problems facing men. This rhetoric has alienated many men who, while sharing some legitimate concerns, do not agree with a stance that directly confronts feminism.

• Men Going Their Way (MGTOW)

This is a movement that advocates for men to "disconnect" from women and the social system that its members claim is designed to oppress men and benefit women. Men in this movement choose to avoid romantic relationships, and in some cases marriage or fatherhood, to protect themselves from what they perceive as a male-hostile culture.

MGTOW argues that contemporary divorce laws, social norms, and gender expectations put men at a disadvantage. Rather than seeking gender equity or reconciliation with feminism, this movement promotes male self-sufficiency and female disengagement as a form of personal empowerment.

The MGTOW movement has gained traction online, where its members share experiences and encourage each other to pursue this lifestyle. However, it has also been criticized for promoting an extreme and pessimistic view of gender relations, often portraying women in a negative light and fostering distrust of them.

• Red Pill and the Manosphere

The concept of the Red Pill comes from the movie The Matrix, in which the protagonist chooses to take a red pill that reveals to him the hidden "truth" of reality. In the context of men's movements, the term Red Pill refers to an ideology that holds that men must "wake up" and see the reality of feminism and contemporary gender dynamics.

The Red Pill is part of the Manosphere, an online ecosystem that includes blogs, forums, and videos where topics related to men's rights, relationships, feminism, and masculinity are discussed. Followers of the Red Pill believe that feminism has manipulated men into submitting to a system that harms them and seeks to restore what they consider the "natural order" of gender relations.

The Red Pill approach tends to be highly critical of feminism and promotes a view of interpersonal relationships in which men should regain control, avoid simply, and focus on their personal development and success. While some in the Manosphere advocate male empowerment, others have been accused of promoting misogynistic ideas and reducing relationships between men and women to power dynamics based on control.

• **"New Masculinity" movements**
In contrast to the more reactive and critical currents towards feminism, movements have also emerged that seek to redefine masculinity in a way that aligns with contemporary values of gender equality and social justice. These movements, often described as part of New Masculinity, promote a way of being a man that is not tied to traditional stereotypes of strength, domination, and emotional control.

New Masculinity advocates for men to feel free to express their emotions, cultivate empathy, and engage in mutually supportive relationships, without the burdens of patriarchal expectations. This approach also invites men to be allies in the fight for gender equality, recognizing that feminism is not an enemy, but an opportunity for men to also break free from rigid gender roles.

Within this movement, initiatives such as HeForShe, promoted by the United Nations, stand out, seeking to involve men in promoting gender equality and women's empowerment. These efforts recognize that the fight for women's rights can also benefit men by challenging the limitations of traditional masculinity.

• Incels (Involuntary Celibates)

Another movement that has gained notoriety, but from a more radical and problematic perspective, is that of the Incels (involuntary celibates). This group is made up of men who feel frustrated by their inability to find sexual or romantic partners and, in many cases, blame women and society in general for their situation. Incels see themselves as victims of a system that prioritizes certain types of men (usually the "alphas") and leaves them marginalized.

The discourse of the Incels is often hostile towards women, whom they accuse of superficiality or of only seeking men with certain physical or social characteristics. Although most incels do not act violently, some members of the community have been linked to incidents of violence, leading to increased media attention and condemnation by other men's movements.

The men's social movements that have emerged in reaction to feminism and the woke movement are diverse and complex. Some seek to confront and resist social changes, while others attempt to find a balance between tradition and contemporary values. While certain groups take more radical and confrontational stances, some currents promote a greater understanding of the challenges men face in modern society, without resorting to misogyny or antagonism.

What is clear is that the debate over masculinity and the role of men in society is far from settled. As gender expectations continue to evolve, we are likely to see a further proliferation of movements attempting to make sense of these changes, some of them pushing for greater equality and others resisting what they perceive as an erosion of traditional values.

Dismantling traditional codes to build a new society

The woke movement represents one of the most potent forces in dismantling the traditional codes that have structured society for centuries. Its focus on intersectionality, social justice, and equity has led to a fundamental re-evaluation of gender norms, race relations, and power dynamics. As societies continue to adapt to the demands of woke, traditional social codes, based on patriarchal domination and rigid hierarchies, are being challenged and redefined. However, it seems that the woke world has overreached itself, trying to force ideas that everything before has been bad, without considering that society has reached this point of evolution by practicing the same model for centuries. Will changing everything not be dangerous?

The future of the woke movement and its impact on society will largely depend on its ability to balance social justice with respect for diversity of opinions and individual freedom.

Chapter 6
Is this the end of chivalry or its rebirth?
Final thoughts

Chivalry, once considered a fundamental pillar in interactions between men and women, has undergone profound transformations throughout history. What began as a code of honor among medieval knights evolved into a set of social norms that dictated the correct way for men to behave toward women and other men. However, in modern society, these norms have been questioned due to changes in gender roles, the evolution of feminism, and the impact of social movements such as woke.

In this final chapter, we will explore whether chivalry has come to an end, or whether it is experiencing a renaissance under new forms that reflect contemporary values of equality, mutual respect, and cooperation. From a historical and sociological perspective, the elements that have contributed to the decline of traditional chivalry and the factors that could be leading to its reinterpretation in the current context will be analyzed.

The Decline of Traditional Chivalry: Historical and Social Factors

Historically, chivalry was tied to power hierarchies and gender roles defined by patriarchal society. In the

Middle Ages, the code of chivalry emerged as a set of values that regulated the behavior of knights, who were not only expected to show bravery and loyalty in battle but also courtesy and respect toward women, particularly toward noble ladies. This behavior was deeply rooted in expectations of protection and provision by men.

However, with the arrival of the Enlightenment and the feminist movements of the twentieth century, these norms began to be questioned. Feminism, particularly in its second and third waves, criticized chivalry as a manifestation of male paternalism, in which the idea that women were weak and in need of male protection was perpetuated. This criticism was accompanied by the growing economic and social independence of women, who demanded equality rather than being treated as fragile or subordinate beings.

Sociologically, the advancement of women's rights, the diversification of families, and the rise of individualism have altered gender dynamics in recent decades. Traditional chivalry, based on a system of rigid roles, lost some of its relevance as society moved towards greater equity and flexibility in gender relations. In this sense, it could be argued that chivalry has been a victim of its rigidity and its inability to adapt to changing times.

Feminism and the resignification of courtesy

Although feminism has questioned chivalry in its traditional form, it has also contributed to a resignification of the concept. Rather than interpreting it as an act of condescension, many voices within modern feminism advocate a new form of courtesy based on mutual respect and gender equality. This resignification implies that both men and women treat each other with dignity and courtesy, without the burden of traditional gender expectations.

For example, modern chivalry no longer revolves around the idea that a man should open the door for a woman, but rather that anyone, regardless of gender, can perform kind gestures toward another. This approach eliminates the implicit hierarchy underlying traditional gender norms and promotes a culture of universal courtesy that recognizes common humanity rather than reinforcing power differentials.

From this perspective, chivalry is not dying but evolving. It is transforming from an exclusively male system of behavior to a set of norms and values that can be practiced by all, with an emphasis on reciprocity, respect, and mutual support.

The revival of chivalry in the contemporary era

Despite social changes that have challenged the foundations of traditional chivalry, there are signs that it may be experiencing a renaissance. This revival is not based on a restoration of old standards of behavior, but on an adaptation of its fundamental principles, respect, courtesy, and support—to new social realities.

Today, many men are revaluing behaviors considered "chivalrous," not as an obligation imposed by society, but as a conscious choice based on principles of respect and empathy. This is reflected in practices such as emotional care, willingness to actively listen, and support in relationships, all without the expectation of dominating or controlling.

The revival of chivalry can also be seen in movements that promote a more balanced masculinity, such as the concept of "new masculinity." This approach moves away from stereotypes of toxic masculinity and promotes the idea that men can be strong and vulnerable at the same time, showing empathy and consideration without losing their sense of identity.

Furthermore, in an increasingly gender-conscious world, modern chivalry is not seen as a series of behaviors that demand something in return, but as a display of respect that can be reciprocated. This means that both men and women can assume chivalrous attitudes without feeling like they are falling into outdated or paternalistic roles.

The downside of chivalry on social media

In the digital age, social media has become a central space for human interaction, transforming the way people connect and relate. Within this environment, complex dynamics have emerged around gender validation and expectations. One phenomenon that has gained notoriety is that of so-called SIMPs, a term used to describe men who, according to this perspective, exhibit excessive submissiveness towards women, especially on online platforms, often in search of approval or recognition. This behavior is closely related to the kind of validation that many women seek on social media, creating a cycle that affects both male and female perceptions of couple relationships.

The term SIMP is derived from English and is an abbreviation of "Simpleton," although, in contemporary popular culture, it has taken on a different meaning. It refers to men who demonstrate excessive devotion or submission towards women, in the hope of receiving attention or affection, although this attention rarely materializes in reciprocity. In many cases, SIMPs are perceived as men who elevate women, often idealizing them, in exchange for crumbs of recognition, such as a "like" on a photo or a superficial comment.

This term has gained popularity on social media, and while it is often used in a joking tone or as a humorous critique, it reflects real behavior that many identify in themselves or others. SIMPs are often seen as people who sacrifice their dignity or self-worth to try to win the favor of women who are often not interested in them romantically.

Social media, such as Instagram, TikTok, or Twitter, has created a space where external validation becomes a central part of the experience. For many people, likes, comments, and followers are a tangible way to measure personal worth or attractiveness, and this search for validation can deeply affect how people perceive themselves and others.

In this context, some women use social media not only to connect with friends and share their lives but also as a platform to gain external validation in the form of male attention. Posting attractive photos, videos, and status updates can be a way to generate a positive response that reinforces their self-esteem and confidence. SIMPs come into play here, as they are often the most active in providing that validation.

SIMPs often flood women's posts with complimentary comments and likes, fueling a cycle of attention in which women receive a constant dose of positive reinforcement. This type of behavior can distort the perception of social and gender interactions. If many men act in this way, women may come to expect all men to respond with the same level of devotion and attention, which can affect how they view romantic relationships outside of social media.

The relationship between SIMPs and seeking validation on social media has a direct impact on how both men and women perceive and behave in their romantic relationships. For women, this constant stream of attention can create unrealistic expectations about what they should expect in a relationship. If they are used to receiving constant, unconditional validation from many men online, they may develop a distorted perception of what a healthy, balanced relationship is, where affection and attention are built on a reciprocal basis.

For SIMPs, this type of behavior can be detrimental to their self-esteem and confidence in the real world. By investing large amounts of time and energy into offering attention and validation that is not reciprocated, SIMPs often end up frustrated and disappointed, which can negatively affect their perception of women and romantic relationships in general. This dynamic creates a cycle of resentment, where men who initially seek approval through submission can become cynical and hostile toward women when their efforts are not rewarded.

This cycle can lead to problems in relationships. Women, accustomed to receiving unbounded attention, may expect the same in a romantic relationship, which can be exhausting or unsustainable for a partner. Similarly, men who act as SIMPs online may struggle to build healthy, balanced relationships in the real world, where mutual respect and reciprocity are key.

Both men and women involved in these dynamics can experience negative effects on their self-esteem and self-concept. For women, while constant online validation may seem positive at first, it can also lead to an unhealthy dependence on outside attention. This search for approval can become a source of anxiety if women begin to define their self-worth solely through the feedback they receive online.

On the other hand, SIMPs, by staking their self-worth on the validation they provide to women, can end up with feelings of inadequacy and rejection when their efforts are not reciprocated. This dependence on female attention can affect their ability to set healthy boundaries and their sense of worth outside of online interaction.

The term SIMP has come under fire for being reductionist and stigmatizing men who show affection or support toward women. While it is true that some men may fall into excessive submissiveness in search of validation, it is also important to recognize that many men simply wish to be kind and respectful. The line between genuine support and submissive idealization can be difficult to define, and the use of the term SIMP can lead to confusion and the disqualification of healthy behaviors of kindness and affection.

At the same time, women who seek validation online also face criticism, as many are accused of "manipulating" or taking advantage of men's attention without offering reciprocation. It is crucial to understand that social media use and validation seeking are common behaviors in the digital age, and do not necessarily imply ill intent.

The relationship between SIMPs and the validation sought by some women on social media reflects a complex dynamic of gender and self-esteem in the digital age. Both parties are caught in a cycle where external validation and submission seem to play a central role in how they interact with each other and how they perceive relationships.

For both men and women to build healthier, more balanced relationships, these dynamics need to be rethought, promoting greater awareness of personal worth that is not dependent on online validation and encouraging reciprocity and mutual respect in romantic interactions. Social media will continue to be an important space for human interaction, but expectations must be based on authenticity rather than submissive or manipulative stereotypes and behaviors.

Chivalry in Modern Times

Chivalry, while often associated with the medieval period, has evolved and adapted over the centuries, maintaining its relevance in contemporary society. Ideals of chivalry, particularly those related to the treatment of women and notions of honor and virtue, have been reinterpreted in modern contexts.

Its influence can be seen in various aspects of modern culture, from literature and film to social norms. The romantic image of knights and their quests continues to captivate audiences, and many contemporary novels and films draw inspiration from chivalric themes. These depictions, while not always historically accurate, contribute to the current fascination with the concept of chivalry and its ideals of heroism and nobility.

The chivalric ideal of serving the greater good has inspired modern movements for social justice. The notion that individuals should use their privilege and power to help others is in tune with the chivalric duty to protect the weak and vulnerable. This connection highlights how chivalric values have adapted to contemporary social dynamics, promoting a sense of responsibility toward the well-being of the community.

In personal relationships, the principles of courtly love, which emphasize respect, affection, and mutual support, can still be observed in modern dating norms. The emphasis on treating partners with dignity and care reflects the lasting impact of chivalric ideals on personal conduct and relationships.

Despite its positive associations, the chivalric ideal has faced criticism in modern discourse. The traditional view of chivalry, especially its role in protecting women, has been scrutinized for its potential ability to perpetuate gender stereotypes. Feminist perspectives argue that while the intention behind chivalry may be noble, it may inadvertently reinforce a narrative in which women are seen as damsels in need of rescue, thereby undermining their agency.

Chivalry and Building Healthy Relationships

One of the most significant aspects of this evolution of chivalry is its role in building healthy relationships. In contemporary society, where individualism and personal autonomy are highly valued, chivalry can play an important role in creating bonds based on mutual respect, open communication, and equal collaboration.

Rather than being seen as a relic of the past, renewed chivalry can help forge more equitable and rewarding relationships, where gestures of courtesy and kindness are not interpreted as forms of superiority, but as expressions of appreciation and care. In this way, chivalry becomes a tool to strengthen human connections rather than reinforce gender inequalities.

Chivalry VS Courtesy

Chivalry and courtesy are concepts that are often used interchangeably but have fundamental differences in their meaning and application. While both involve behaviors that denote respect and consideration for others, chivalry has a specific focus on the relationship between men and women, rooted in historical and social norms, while courtesy is a general behavior of good treatment that extends to all people, regardless of gender. In this final section, we will explore these differences, their origin, and how they manifest today.

• **Origin and definition of chivalry**

As we have mentioned in previous chapters, chivalry has its roots in the Middle Ages, when knights were prominent figures who represented a strict code of conduct. This code not only covered martial skills and loyalty to the feudal lord, but also honorable behavior toward women, which involved protection, deference, and respect. This special treatment was linked to the idea that women should be cared for and protected since they were perceived as more vulnerable and in need of male protection.

Over the centuries, this concept of chivalry evolved but retained its focus on a man's treatment of a woman. Gestures such as offering a lady a handkerchief, offering her his coat, paying the bill on a date, or giving up his seat are classic examples of chivalrous behavior that still prevail in contemporary culture. While these acts may be considered an expression of respect, they are also based on the presumption that women somehow require special or differentiated treatment than would be granted to a man.

Chivalry, in this sense, can be seen as behavior that maintains certain traditional gender roles, in which the man is the protector, and the woman is protected. While many of these gestures may seem kind and respectful, they have sparked debates in the context of gender equality. Some people view chivalry as a form of condescension or paternalism, while others value these gestures as expressions of politeness and respect.

• Origin and definition of courtesy

On the other hand, courtesy is a broader concept that is not restricted by gender or traditional roles. Courtesy refers to the practice of showing consideration, kindness, and respect towards all people, regardless of their gender, status, or relationship. Its origin comes from the social norms that regulated behavior in royal and aristocratic courts, where people were expected to follow certain standards of etiquette and good treatment in their everyday interactions.

Today, courtesy manifests itself in small, everyday actions that show respect and consideration for others. These gestures include saying "please" and "thank you," waiting patiently in a line, giving way, helping someone in need, or simply saying hello in a friendly manner. Courtesy does not have a particular bias toward any gender, nor does it suggest that a person should be treated differently because of their sex. At its core, courtesy is based on a sense of mutual respect and the idea that everyone deserves to be treated with dignity.

Likewise, being polite offers emotional control, since, when faced with insults, a person can measure his anger and respond calmly.

Key differences between chivalry and courtesy

Gender focus: Chivalry is centered on the man's treatment of women. It has a strong historical basis in traditional gender roles, where the man acts as a protector and the woman is seen as the person to be protected or assisted.

Courtesy, on the other hand, is gender neutral. It applies to anyone and does not presuppose that someone should receive special treatment based on their sex. It is a general manifestation of respect and good manners toward all.

Underlying intention: Chivalry implies a protective or helpful intention of the man toward the woman. Although it may be born from a desire to be considerate, it also reflects a traditional perception of the relationship between genders.

Courtesy, on the other hand, is based on a broader intention of respect toward all. It does not assume that someone needs attention based on their gender, but that everyone deserves to be treated with dignity.

Traditional vs. contemporary social norms: Chivalry, as mentioned above, is based on older social norms that have been challenged in the modern era, especially in the context of feminism and gender equality movements. While many appreciate these gestures, others see them as perpetuating unequal gender roles.

Courtesy, on the other hand, remains a universally appreciated value in society

Radical feminism's view on courtesy

Regarding courtesy, which is more general and does not focus on specific treatment between men and women, radical feminists tend to be less critical, as courtesy is a behavior that applies to all people equally. However, even here there can be nuances. For example, a man who "excessively" offers help to a woman can be interpreted as someone who is acting under the premise that she cannot solve problems on her own.

For radical feminism, it is not so much the gesture itself that is important, but the intention and context. If the act of courtesy assumes of inequality or the belief that women are inherently different and more vulnerable than men, it may be rejected as a way of reaffirming those differences.

Consequences on male behavior

The criticism of chivalry by sectors of radical feminism has had a notable impact on the behavior of many men. These impacts can vary depending on the environment and the degree of exposure to feminist ideas. Some of the main consequences include:

<u>Confusion and uncertainty in social interactions:</u> Many men today find themselves at a crossroads, not knowing whether certain gestures of courtesy or chivalry will be well received or misinterpreted. Simply opening a door or giving up a seat can cause uncertainty, as men do not wish to appear condescending, disrespectful, or SIMPs. This situation

has led some to choose to avoid these traditional acts altogether, fearing a negative reaction. For example, the street compliment has disappeared, for fear that women will report them for harassment.

<u>Self-censorship and withdrawal:</u> Faced with criticism of chivalry, some men have opted to self-censor their behavior, preferring not to interact with women in ways that were previously considered polite or appropriate. This self-censorship can lead to social withdrawal, in which some men feel less inclined to offer help, either for fear of offending or because of the idea that their gesture will be interpreted as an attempt to impose superiority.

<u>Redefinition of respect and good manners:</u> In some cases, feminist criticism has led to a redefinition of respect and courtesy in relationships between men and women. Increasingly, there is a search for equal treatment based on mutual respect, without gestures that reinforce traditional gender roles. For example, instead of offering a seat or opening a door specifically for a woman, the idea of being polite to everyone, regardless of gender, is emphasized.

<u>Polarization of behaviors:</u> On the other hand, this criticism has also generated an opposite reaction in certain groups of men, who openly reject the ideas of radical feminism and defend chivalry as a positive value and as part of their masculine identity. This rejection of feminist criticism can lead to polarization, where some men see chivalry as reaffirming their traditional beliefs about the role of men in society.

Repercussions on relationships between men and women

The debate on chivalry has generated tensions in relationships between men and women, particularly in social and work contexts. Some men may feel discouraged when trying to interact with women, fearing that their gestures will be misinterpreted, while some women may see these changes as a loss of politeness or even as a lack of respect.

On the other hand, many women who do not identify with radical feminism may still appreciate chivalrous gestures and lament the decline of these behaviors in everyday life. This can create a disconnect between what some men believe is right (avoiding behaviors that may be seen as patronizing) and what some women value in their interactions with men.

Radical feminist critique of chivalry has highlighted existing tensions between traditional gender roles and contemporary ideals of equality. While for some these gestures are an expression of respect and kindness, for others they are a perpetuation of power dynamics that must be dismantled. The consequences for male behavior vary, from self-censorship to rejection of these ideas, creating a complex landscape in relationships between men and women.

Ultimately, the challenge is to find a balance where men can show respect and kindness without falling into patterns that reinforce unequal gender stereotypes, and where both men and women feel valued and respected in their daily interactions.

Final Thoughts: The End or Rebirth of Chivalry?

The debate over whether chivalry has come to an end or is experiencing a revival reflects the broader tensions between tradition and social change. While some consider chivalry, in its traditional form, to be outdated in a society that values gender equality, others argue that its core principles can be updated to fit contemporary values.

From a sociological perspective, chivalry has not disappeared entirely; it has simply changed form. Rather than adhering to rigid gender-based standards of behavior, modern chivalry is based on mutual respect, empathy, and reciprocity. Thus, far from being a dying concept, chivalry is finding new ways to manifest itself in contemporary society.

Ultimately, the future of chivalry will depend on our ability to adapt it to new social realities. While the patriarchal structures that once underpin traditional chivalry are in decline, the values of courtesy, respect, and mutual support remain relevant and necessary in human relationships.

———†———

www.ingramcontent.com/pod-product-compliance
Lightning Source LLC
Chambersburg PA
CBHW061351140726
47997CB00003B/1157